Emerson on Swedenborg: introducing the Mystic

Emerson on Swedenborg: introducing the Mystic

by
Ralph Waldo Emerson

Edited and introduced by Stephen McNeilly

The Swedenborg Society
Swedenborg House
20-21 Bloomsbury Way
London WC1A 2TH

———

2003

ACKNOWLEDGEMENTS

Many thanks to Victoria Gordon, Emma Keast,
Richard Lines, Paul McNeilly and Lara Muth.

Published by:
The Swedenborg Society
Swedenborg House
20-21 Bloomsbury Way
London WC1A 2TH

Edited by Stephen McNeilly
Assistant Editor: James Wilson

Typeset at Swedenborg House.
Printed and bound in Great Britain at Biddles.

ISBN 0 85448 139 7
British Library Cataloguing-in-Publication Data.
A catalogue record for this book is available
from the British Library.

Table of Contents

Table of Contents

——

——

Introduction

by Stephen McNeilly

'After Dante, Shakespeare and Milton there came no grand poet until
Swedenborg sung the wonders of man's heart in strange prose poems
which he called *Heaven and Hell*, the *Apocalypse Revealed*, the
Doctrine of Marriage, *Celestial Secrets* and so on...'
—Ralph Waldo Emerson[1]

S*wedenborg; or the Mystic* is one of a collection of seven lectures
published in 1850 by Ralph Waldo Emerson entitled *Representative
Men*.[2] The other six lectures are: *Plato, or the Philosopher*;
Montaigne, or the Sceptic; *Shakespeare, or the Poet*; *Napoleon, or the Man
of the World*; *Goethe, or the Writer*; and an introductory lecture entitled *The
Uses of Great Men*.

The lecture on Swedenborg was first given on Christmas Day in Boston,
1845, and was repeated in Manchester in 1847.[3] It was, by all accounts, a
great success. Samuel Longfellow recalled that the theatre in Boston was
full with 'old men and young, bald heads and flowing transcendental locks,
matrons and maidens, misanthropists and lovers',[4] and a correspondent
for the *Howitt's Journal* of 1847 (Manchester), wrote:

'[the lecture] emerged like a golden mist around a setting sun,—you
perceived nothing but splendid words without anything definite at first;

but, by-and-bye, one object after another came clear...invested with a glory from the medium through which they passed...and then wandering far away into the mystical theories of Swedenborg...no orator ever succeeded with so little exertion in entrancing his audience, stealing away each faculty, and leading the listeners captive to his will...The moment he finished he took up his MS, and quietly glided away,— disappearing before his audience could give vent to their applause'.[5]

It was soon to become a classic. Clarence Hotson, in 1929, wrote that this text had done 'more than any other to make the name of Emanuel Swedenborg known to the world'.[6] And Jorge Luis Borges, some 50 years later, indicated its continued importance by utilising its premise as a counterpoint for his own essay on Swedenborg.[7]

*

Although written in the manner of a 'biographical sketch', Emerson's reasons for writing *Swedenborg, or the Mystic* were primarily philosophical. His first strategy—within the specific context of *Representative Men*—was to show how Swedenborg represented the moral/ethical middle ground between the scepticism of Montaigne and the idealism of Plato. 'The moral insights' of a man like Swedenborg, Emerson writes, put him in higher esteem than any other modern writer: 'For other things I make poetry of them; but the moral sentiment makes poetry of me'.[8] This alone, he suggests, 'entitle[s] him to a place, vacant for some ages among the lawgivers of mankind'.[9]

His second strategy, however—and stretching beyond the context of *Representative Men*—was to offer comment on Swedenborg's vast methodological system entitled the Science of Correspondences.[10] Digressions in earlier essays on this doctrine had shown him to be an enthusiastic supporter of Swedenborg. In his Harvard address of 1836, for example, his endorsement was unequivocal. 'There is one man of genius', he writes,

> 'who has done much for this philosophy of life, whose literary value has never yet been rightly estimated;——I mean Emanuel Swedenborg...[This] most imaginative of men...writing with the precision of a mathematician, endeavoured to engraft a purely philosophical Ethics on the popular Christianity of his time...he saw and showed the connection between nature and the affections of the soul. He pierced the emblematic or spiritual character of the visible, audible, tangible world. Especially did his shade-loving muse hover over and interpret the lower parts of nature; he showed the mysterious bond that allies moral evil to the foul material forms, and has given in epical parables a theory of insanity, of beasts, of unclean and fearful things'.[11]

In turn, the quotation given at the beginning of this 'Introduction', first printed in his 1841 essay 'The Poet', is equally supportive.

It is Emerson's suggestion that it is the moral insight that brings nature to life, and it is the animation of this insight that connects the creator to his creation. If 'adequately executed', he writes, the Science of Correspondences 'would be the poem of the world', in which all science and morality would play a part.[12] Emerson's aim, as such, in *Swedenborg, or the Mystic*, is to reconcile the one (science) to the other (morality).

*

The current edition—published separately, and for the first time, with full critical apparatus—has the advantage of previous versions in that it contains a *Glossary of names cited*, a concise *Chronology* of both Swedenborg and Emerson and an *Index*. The text has also undergone some modification. In an attempt to render Emerson's 19th century prose more accessible to a 21st century audience, many of Emerson's long paragraphs have been amended and the text itself has been divided into nine parts. Emerson's original title for this essay, *Swedenborg, or the Mystic*, has also been revised to *Emerson on Swedenborg: introducing the Mystic*. Emerson's meaning for the term 'Mystic' can be understood in the sense used by Swedenborg in his *Arcana Caelestia,* i.e. as one who receives knowledge of the Divine from a source higher than experience.[13]

Emerson's views on Swedenborg, over the years, have been subject to much debate from scholars of both men.[14] In closing, I would like to cite a poem published by Emerson in 1867, seventeen years after the first publication of *Representative Men*:

Far in the North, where polar night
Holds in check the frolic light,
In trance upborne past mortal goal
The Swede EMANUEL leads the soul.
Through snows above, mines underground,
The inks of Erebus he found;
Rehearsed to men the damned wails
On which the seraph music sails.
In spirit-worlds he trod alone,
But walked the earth unmarked, unknown.
The near bystander caught no sound, —

Introduction

———

Yet they who listened far aloof
Heard rendings of the skyey roof,
And felt, beneath, the quaking ground;
And his air-sown, unheeded words,
In the next age, are flaming swords.[15]

Readers wishing to explore Emerson's views further might consult the introduction to volume IV of *The Collected Works of Ralph Waldo Emerson*, published by Belknap Press of Harvard University Press (1986). For a good introduction to the thought of Swedenborg see *introducing the New Jerusalem* published by The Swedenborg Society (2003).

NOTES

[1] *The Poet*. Ralph Waldo Emerson, 1841. Walt Whitman, who attended this lecture, desribed it as 'the richest and most beautiful composition, both in its manner and style, we have ever heard anywhere, at anytime'. *Walt Whitman of the New York Aurora, Editor at Twenty-Two: A Collection of Recently Discovered Writings*. Edited by J J Rubin & C H Brown. Pennsylvania State College: Bald Eagle Press. (1950). Page 105.

[2] The current popular edition of Emerson's *Representative Men* is published by Harvard University Press (1996) with an introduction by Andrew Delbanco.

[3] For historical and textual information on Emerson's *Representative Men* please see W E Williams' introduction to vol. IV of *The Collected Works of Ralph Waldo Emerson*, published by Belknap Press of Harvard University Press (1986).

[4] 'Introduction' to Emerson's *Representative Men*. Page vii. Andrew Delbanco. Harvard University Press (1996).

[5] See note 3 above, page xlvii.

[6] 'Emerson's Title for "Swedenborg"'. Clarence Hotson. *New Church Life*. (July 1929).

[7] This essay has recently been republished by The Swedenborg Society as an 'Introduction' to Swedenborg's *The Spiritual Diary* Vol. 1 (2002).

[8] See page 2 of this volume.

———

[9] See page 33 of this volume.

[10] The *Science of Correspondences* is, perhaps, the most famous of Swedenborg's doctrines. It is Swedenborg's claim that all material things are representative of spiritual principles. In *Nature* (1836), and paraphrasing Swedenborg's *Science of Correspondences*, Emerson wrote:

'Every natural fact is a symbol of some spiritual fact. Every appearance in nature corresponds to some state of the mind, and that state of mind can only be described by presenting that natural appearance as a picture. An enraged man is a lion, a cunning man is a fox, a firm man is a rock...a lamb is innocence'.

According to Swedenborg, this finds its fullest expression in *The Word*, which consists of many texts from the Old and New Testaments.

[11] *The American Scholar*. Harvard address of 1836. Interestingly, this lecture marked Emerson's first meeting with Henry David Thoreau.

[12] See page 29 of this volume.

[13] Emerson's description of Swedenborg as a 'Mystic' has caused some controversy since its publication. The most vocal response coming from George Bush who published a twenty-eight page pamphlet entitled *Prof. Bush's Reply to Ralph Waldo Emerson on Swedenborg*. Bush's main concern was that the term 'Mystic' might diminish the revelatory claims of Swedenborg's works and imply (in accordance with the popular understanding at the time) someone who was 'self-deluded' or prone to 'self-indulgent' mystification. Emerson's intentions, however, were quite different. All the evidence suggests that Emerson's view was close to Swedenborg's as given in his *Arcana Caelestia* §4923.2. For the sake of clarity, the relevelant sections of this passage are as follows:

'[...]because the Word is Divine, the mystical meaning within it must of necessity be the kind of meaning the angels in heaven understand, and that the Word cannot have any other mystical content[...] This mystical meaning understood by the angels in heaven is nothing else than what is called spiritual and celestial, the sole subject which is the Lord [...and] because in the Lord's Divine mercy I have been allowed to be simultaneously in heaven as a spirit and on earth as a man, and consequently to talk to angels, doing so now without a break for many years, what else can I do but disclose those things which are called the mystical contents of the Word, that is, its interiors, which are the spiritual and celestial things of the Lord's Kingdom'.

[14] See, in particular Anders Hallengren's 'The Importance of Swedenborg to Emerson's Ethics'. *Swedenborg and his Influence*. The Academy of the New Church, (1988).

[15] 'Solution'. First published in *May-Day and Other Poems*, (1867).

—

Chronology of Swedenborg's life and works

1688—January 29, born Emanuel Swedberg.

1696—Emanuel's mother, Sara Behm, dies June 17.

1709—Emanuel graduates from Uppsala University.

1710—First trip abroad.

1714—Finishes drawings of various inventions, including a water clock and submarine.

1715—Publishes the first issues of the scientific journal *Daedalus Hyperboreus*.

1719—Family ennoblement and change of name to Swedenborg.

1723—Swedenborg appointed Extraordinary Assessor by the Board of Mines. Emanuel's father, Bishop Jesper Swedberg, dies.

1734—Publishes his major philosophical and scientific work the *Principia*.

1740-42—Publishes *Oeconomia Regni Animalis*.

1743-44—First addressed by a spirit. Writes his *Journal of Dreams*.

1744—Publishes *Regnum Animale*.

1747—Resigns from Board of Mines.

1749-56—Publishes his major work *Arcana Caelestia*, a biblical exegesis in eight Latin volumes.

1757—Writes of the Last Judgment in the spirit-world.

1758—Whilst in London, Swedenborg publishes *Heaven and Hell, Worlds in Space, Last Judgment, New Jerusalem and its Heavenly Doctrine* and *The White Horse*.

1763—Publishes *Divine Love and Wisdom*.

1764—Publishes *Divine Providence*.

1766—Publishes *Apocalyspe Revealed*. Immanuel Kant publishes his attack on Swedenborg entitled *Dreams of a Spirit-Seer*.

1768—Publishes *Conjugial Love*.

1769—Publishes *The Interaction of the Soul and Body*.

1770—Swedenborg appeals to King Adolf Frederic regarding the controversy in Sweden surrounding his *Conjugial Love*.

1771—Publishes *The True Christian Religion*. In the same year, Swedenborg suffers a stroke but partially recovers.

1772—Writes to John Wesley. On Sunday, March 29, Swedenborg dies.

Chronology of Emerson's life and works

1803——Born May 25 in Boston.

1811——Father, William Emerson, dies.

1829——Ordained as junior minister of Second Church (Unitarian) in Boston, and marries Ellen Tucker.

1831——Wife Ellen dies.

1832——Resigns from Second Church. Undertakes his first trip to Italy, France, England and Scotland.

1833——Meets S T Coleridge, W Wordsworth and T Carlyle.

1834——Settles in Concord.

1835——Marries Lidian (Lydia) Jackson.

1835——*Nature* published.

1837——Gives 'The American Scholar' address at Harvard. Henry David Thoreau is in attendance. Writes *The Concord Hymn*.

1841——*Essays* (first series) published including 'Self-Reliance' and 'The Over-Soul'. Thoreau moves into Emerson's home for two-year stay.

———

1842——Lectures in New York, meets Henry James and assumes editorship of *The Dial*.

1844——*Essays: Second Series* published. Delivers first public statement against slavery.

1845——Henry David Thoreau moves into self-built cabin on Emerson's property. Emerson gives lecture series *Representative Men*.

1846——Poems published.

1847-48——Second trip to England and France, British lecture tour. Visits Thomas Carlyle and William Wordsworth.

1850——*Representative Men* published.

1851——Speaks on the Fugitive Slave Law.

1852——Emerson's mother, Ruth Haskins Emerson, dies at 85, at Emerson's home.

1854——Meets Walt Whitman in New York.

1856——*English Traits* published.

1860——*The Conduct of Life* published.

1862——Meets Abraham Lincoln. Henry David Thoreau dies. Emerson gives funeral oration.

1870——*Society and Solitude* published.

1874——*Parnassus* published.

1875——*Letters and Social Aims* published.

1882——Emerson dies in Concord on April 27, at age 78.

1884——*Lectures and Biographical Sketches* and *Miscellanies* published.

1893——*Natural History of the Intellect* and *Other Papers* published.

_____

Emerson on Swedenborg:
introducing the Mystic

| Part One |

A mong eminent persons, those who are most dear to men are not of the class which the economist calls producers: they have nothing in their hands; they have not cultivated corn, nor made bread; they have not led out a colony, nor invented a loom.

A higher class in the estimation and love of this city-building market-going race of mankind, are the poets, who, from the intellectual kingdom, feed the thought and imagination with ideas and pictures which raise men out of the world of corn and money, and console them for the shortcomings of the day and the meanness of labour and traffic.

Then also the philosopher has his value, who flatters the intellect of this labourer by engaging him with subtleties which instruct him in new faculties. Others may build cities; he is to understand them and keep them in awe. But there is a class who lead us into another region——the world of morals or of will. What is singular about this region of thought is its claim. Wherever the sentiment of right comes in, it takes precedence of everything else. For other things I make poetry of them; but the moral sentiment makes poetry of me.

I have sometimes thought that he would render the greatest service to modern criticism, who should draw the line of relation that subsists between Shakespeare and Swedenborg. The human mind stands ever in perplexity, demanding intellect, demanding sanctity, impatient equally of each without the other. The reconciler has not yet appeared. If we tire of the saints, Shakespeare is our city of refuge. Yet the instincts presently teach that the problem of Essence must take precedence of all others——the questions of Whence? What? and Whither? and the solution of these must be in a life, and not in a book.

A drama or poem is a proximate or oblique reply; but Moses, Menu, Jesus, work directly on this problem. The atmosphere of moral sentiment is a region of grandeur which reduces all material mag-nificence to toys, yet opens to every wretch that has reason, the doors of the universe. Almost with a fierce haste it lays its empire on the man. In the language of the Koran,

> 'God said, the heaven and the earth and all that is between them, think ye that we created them in jest, and that ye shall not return to us?' [1]

It is the kingdom of the will, and by inspiring the will, which is the

——

seat of personality, seems to convert the universe into a person;

'The realms of being to no other bow,
Not only all are thine, but all are Thou'.[2]

All men are commanded by the saint. The Koran makes a distinct
class of those who are by nature good, and whose goodness has an
influence on others, and pronounces this class to be the aim of
creation: the other classes are admitted to the feast of being, only as
following in the train of this. And the Persian poet exclaims to a soul
of this kind;

'Go boldly forth, and feast on being's banquet;
Thou art the called——the rest admitted with thee'.[3]

The privilege of this caste is an access to the secrets and structure
of nature by some higher method than by experience. In common
parlance, what one man is said to learn by experience, a man of
extraordinary sagacity is said, without experience, to divine. The
Arabians say, that Abul Khair, the mystic, and Abu Ali Seena, the
philosopher, conferred together; and, on parting, the philosopher said,
"All that he sees, I know"; and the mystic said, "All that he knows, I
see".[4] If one should ask the reason of this intuition, the solution would
lead us into that property which Plato denoted as Reminiscence, and
which is implied by the Bramins in the tenet of Transmigration. The

——

soul having been often born, or, as the Hindus say, 'travelling the path of existence through thousands of births',[5] having beheld the things which are here, those which are in heaven and those which are beneath, there is nothing of which she has not gained the know-ledge: no wonder that she is able to recollect, in regard to any one thing, what formerly she knew.

> 'For, all things in nature being linked and related, and the soul having heretofore known all, nothing hinders but that any man who has recalled to mind, or according to the common phrase has learned, one thing only, should of himself recover all his ancient knowledge, and find out again all the rest, if he have but courage and faint not in the midst of his researches. For inquiry and learning is reminiscence all.'[6]

How much more, if he that inquires be a holy and godlike soul. For by being assimilated to the original Soul, by whom and after whom all things subsist, the soul of man does then easily flow into all things, and all things flow into it: they mix; and he is present and sympathetic with their structure and law.

This path is difficult, secret and beset with terror. The ancients called it *ecstasy* or absence—a getting out of their bodies to think. All re-ligious history contains traces of the trance of saints—a beatitude, but without any sign of joy; earnest, solitary, even sad; 'the flight', Plotinus called it, 'of the alone to the alone';[7] Μύεσις, the closing of the eyes—whence our word, Mystic. The trances of Socrates, Plotinus, Porphyry, Behmen, Bunyan, Fox, Pascal, Guyon, Swedenborg, will readily come to mind. But what as readily comes to mind is the accompaniment of disease. This beatitude comes in terror, and with shocks to the mind of the receiver;

'It o'er informs the tenement of clay'[8]

and drives the man mad, or gives a certain violent bias which taints his judgment. In the chief examples of religious illumination somewhat morbid has mingled, in spite of the unquestionable increase of mental power. Must the highest good drag after it a quality which neutralizes and discredits it?

'Indeed, it takes
From our achievements, when performed at height
The pith and marrow of our attribute.'[9]

Shall we say, that the economical mother disburses so much earth and so much fire, by weight and metre, to make a man, and will not add a pennyweight, though a nation is perishing for a leader? Therefore the men of God purchased their science by folly or pain. If you will have pure carbon, carbuncle, or diamond, to make the brain transparent, the trunk and organs shall be so much the grosser: instead of porcelain they are potter's earth, clay, or mud.

| Part Two |

I n modern times no such remarkable example of this introverted mind has occurred as in Emanuel Swedenborg, born
in Stockholm, in 1688.

This man, who appeared to his contemporaries a visionary and
elixir of moonbeams, no doubt led the most real life of any man
then in the world: and now when the royal and ducal Frederics, Cristierns and Brunswicks of that day have slid into oblivion, he begins to
spread himself into the minds of thousands.

As happens in great men, he seemed by the variety and amount of
his powers to be a composition of several persons, like the giant fruits
which are matured in gardens by the union of four or five single blos-
soms. His frame is on a larger scale and possesses the advantages of
size. As it is easier to see the reflection of the great sphere in large globes,
though defaced by some crack or blemish, than in drops of water, so
men of large calibre, though with some eccentricity or madness, like

———

Pascal or Newton, help us more than balanced mediocre minds.

His youth and training could not fail to be extraordinary. Such a boy could not whistle or dance, but goes grubbing into mines and mountains, prying into chemistry and optics, physiology, mathematics and astronomy, to find images fit for the measure of his versatile and capacious brain. He was a scholar from a child, and was educated at Uppsala.

At the age of twenty-eight he was made Assessor of the Board of Mines by Charles XII. In 1716, he left home for four years and visited the universities of England, Holland, France and Germany. He performed a notable feat of engineering in 1718, at the siege of Fredericshall, by hauling two galleys, five boats and a sloop, some fourteen English miles overland, for the royal service. In 1721 he journeyed over Europe to examine mines and smelting works. He published in 1716 his *Daedalus Hyperboreus*,[10] and from this time for the next thirty years was employed in the composition and publication of his scientific works. With the like force he threw himself into theology.

In 1743, when he was fifty-four years old, what is called his illumination began. All his metallurgy and transportation of ships overland was absorbed into this ecstasy. He ceased to publish any more scientific books, withdrew from his practical labours and devoted himself to the writing and publication of his voluminous theological works, which were printed at his own expense, or at that of the Duke of Brunswick or other prince, at Dresden, Leipsic, London, or Amsterdam.

Later, he resigned his office of Assessor: the salary attached to this

———

———

office continued to be paid to him during his life. His duties had brought him into intimate acquaintance with King Charles XII, by whom he was much consulted and honoured. The like favour was continued to him by his successor. At the Diet of 1751, Count Hopken says the most solid memorials on Finance were from his pen. In Sweden he appears to have attracted a marked regard. His rare science and practical skill, and the added fame of second sight and extraordinary religious knowledge and gifts, drew to him queens, nobles, clergy, shipmasters and people about the ports through which he was wont to pass in his many voyages.

The clergy interfered a little with the importation and publication of his religious works, but he seems to have kept the friendship of men in power. He was never married. He had great modesty and gentleness of bearing. His habits were simple; he lived on bread, milk and vegetables. He lived in a house situated in a large garden; he went several times to England where he does not seem to have attracted any attention whatever from the learned or the eminent; and died at London, March 29, 1772, of apoplexy, in his eighty-fifth year. He is described, when in London, as a man of a quiet, clerical habit, not averse to tea and coffee, and kind to children.

He wore a sword when in full velvet dress, and, whenever he walked out, carried a gold-headed cane. There is a common portrait of him in antique coat and wig, but the face has a wandering or vacant air.

The genius which was to penetrate the science of the age with a far more subtle science; to pass the bounds of space and time, venture

———

into the dim spirit-realm, and attempt to establish a new religion in the world——began its lessons in quarries and forges, in the smelting-pot and crucible, in ship-yards and dissecting-rooms.

No one man is perhaps able to judge of the merits of his works on so many subjects. One is glad to learn that his books on mines and metals are held in the highest esteem by those who understand these matters. It seems that he anticipated much science of the nineteenth century; anticipated, in astronomy, the discovery of the seventh planet ——but, unhappily, not also of the eighth; anticipated the views of modern astronomy in regard to the generation of earths by the sun; in magnetism, some important experiments and conclusions of later students; in chemistry, the atomic theory; in anatomy, the discoveries of Schlichting, Monro and Wilson; and first demonstrated the office of the lungs. His excellent English editor magnanimously lays no stress on his discoveries, since he was too great to care to be original; and we are to judge, by what he can spare, of what remains.

A colossal soul, he lies vast abroad on his times, uncomprehended by them, and requires a long focal distance to be seen; suggests, as Aristotle, Bacon, Selden, Humboldt, that a certain vastness of learning, or *quasi* omnipresence of the human soul in nature is possible. His superb speculation, as from a tower, over nature and arts, without ever losing sight of the texture and sequence of things, almost realises his own picture, in the *Principia*,[11] of the original integrity of man. Over and above the merit of his particular discoveries, is the capital merit of his self-equality. A drop of water has the properties of the sea, but cannot exhibit a storm. There is beauty of a concert, as well as of a flute; strength of a host, as well as of a hero; and, in Swedenborg, those who are best acquainted with modern books will most admire the merit of mass.

One of the missouriums and mastodons of literature, he is not to be measured by whole colleges of ordinary scholars. His stalwart presence would flutter the gowns of an university. Our books are false by being fragmentary: their sentences are *bon mots*, and not parts of natural discourse; childish expressions of surprise or pleasure in nature; or, worse, owing a brief notoriety to their petulance, or aversion from the order of nature—being some curiosity or oddity, designedly not in harmony with nature and purposely framed to excite surprise, as jugglers do by concealing their means.

But Swedenborg is systematic and respective of the world in every sentence: all the means are orderly given; his faculties work with astronomic punctuality, and this admirable writing is pure from all pertness or egotism.

Part Three

S wedenborg was born into an atmosphere of great ideas. It is hard to say what was his own: yet his life was dignified by noblest pictures of the universe.

The robust Aristotelian method, with its breadth and adequateness, shaming our sterile and linear logic by its genial radiation, conversant with series and degree, with effects and ends, skilful to discriminate power from form, essence from accident, and opening, by its terminology and definition, high roads into nature, had trained a race of athletic philosophers.

Harvey had shown the circulation of the blood; Gilbert had shown that the earth was a magnet; Descartes, taught by Gilbert's magnet, with its vortex, spiral and polarity, had filled Europe with the leading thought of vortical motion, as the secret of nature. Newton, in the year in which Swedenborg was born, published the *Principia*,[12] and established the Universal Gravity. Malpighi, following the high doctrines of

---

Hippocrates, Leucippus and Lucretius, had given emphasis to the dogma that nature works in leasts—'*tota in minimis existit natura*'.[13] Unrivalled dissectors, Swammerdam, Leeuwenhoek, Winslow, Eustachius, Heister, Vesalius, Boerhaave, had left nothing for scalpel or microscope to reveal in human or comparative anatomy: Linnaeus, his contemporary, was affirming, in his beautiful science, that 'Nature is always like herself';[14] and, lastly, the nobility of method, the largest application of principles, had been exhibited by Leibnitz and Christian Wolff, in cosmology; whilst Locke and Grotius had drawn the moral argument.

What was left for a genius of the largest calibre but to go over their ground and verify and unite? It is easy to see in these minds the origin of Swedenborg's studies, and the suggestion of his problems. He had a capacity to entertain and vivify these volumes of thought. Yet the proximity of these geniuses, one or other of whom had introduced all his leading ideas, makes Swedenborg another example of the difficulty, even in a highly fertile genius, of proving originality, the first birth and annunciation of one of the laws of nature.

He named his favourite views the doctrine of Forms, the doctrine of Series and Degrees, the doctrine of Influx, the doctrine of Correspondence. His statement of these doctrines deserves to be studied in his books. Not every man can read them, but they will reward him who can. His theologic works are valuable to illustrate these. His writings would be a sufficient library to a lonely and athletic student; and the *Economy of the Animal Kingdom*[15] is one of those books which by the sustained dignity of thinking is an honour to the human race.

He had studied spars and metals to some purpose. His varied and solid knowledge makes his style lustrous with points and shooting spicula of thought, and resembling one of those winter mornings when the air sparkles with crystals. The grandeur of the topics makes the grandeur of the style. He was apt for cosmology, because of that native perception of identity which made mere size of no account to him. In the atom of magnetic iron he saw the quality which would generate the spiral motion of sun and planet.

The thoughts in which he lived were, the universality of each law in nature; the Platonic doctrine of the scale or degrees; the version or conversion of each into other, and so the correspondence of all the parts; the fine secret that little explains large, and large, little; the centrality of man in nature, and the connection that subsists throughout all things. He saw that the human body was strictly universal, or an instrument through which the soul feeds and is fed by the whole of matter; so that he held, in exact antagonism to the skeptics, that 'the wiser a man is, the more will he be a worshipper of the Deity'.[16]

In short, he was a believer in the Identity-philosophy which he held not idly, as the dreamers of Berlin or Boston, but which he experimented with through years of labour, with the heart and strength of the rudest Viking that his rough Sweden ever sent to battle.

This theory dates from the oldest philosophers, and derives perhaps its best illustration from the newest. It is this, that nature iterates her means perpetually on successive planes. In the old aphorism, *Nature is always self-similar*.[17] In the plant, the eye or germinative point opens to a leaf, then to another leaf, with a power of transforming the leaf into radicle, stamen, pistil, petal, bract, sepal, or seed.

The whole art of the plant is still to repeat leaf on leaf without end, the more or less of heat, light, moisture and food determining the form it shall assume. In the animal, nature makes a vertebra, or a spine of vertebrae, and helps herself still by a new spine, with a limited power of modifying its form——spine on spine, to the end of the world.

A poetic anatomist in our own day teaches that a snake, being a horizontal line, and man, being an erect line, constitute a right angle; and between the lines of this mystical quadrant all animated beings find their place: and he assumes the hair-worm, the span-worm, or the snake, as the type or prediction of the spine.

Manifestly, at the end of the spine, nature puts out smaller spines, as arms; at the end of the arms, new spines, as hands; at the other end, she repeats the process, as legs and feet. At the top of the column she puts out another spine, which doubles or loops itself over, as a span-worm, into a ball, and forms the skull, with extremities again: the hands being now the upper jaw, the feet the lower jaw, the fingers and toes being represented this time by upper and lower teeth.

This new spine is destined to high uses. It is a new man on the shoulders of the last. It can almost shed its trunk and manage to live alone, according to the Platonic idea in the *Timaeus*.[18] Within it, on a higher plane, all that was done in the trunk repeats itself. Nature recites her lesson once more in a higher mood. The mind is a finer body, and resumes its functions of feeding, digesting, absorbing, excluding and generating, in a new and ethereal element.

Here in the brain is all the process of alimentation repeated, in the acquiring, comparing, digesting and assimilating of experience. Here again is the mystery of generation repeated. In the brain are male and female faculties; here is marriage, here is fruit. And there is no limit to this ascending scale but series on series. Everything, at the end of one use, is taken up into the next, each series punctually repeating every organ and process of the last. We are adapted to infinity. We are hard to please, and love nothing which ends; and in nature is no end, but everything at the end of one use is lifted into a superior, and the ascent of these things climbs into daemonic and celestial natures. Creative force, like a musical composer, goes on unweariedly repeating a simple air or theme, now high, now low, in solo, in chorus, ten thousand times reverberated, till it fills earth and heaven with the chant.

| Part Four |

Gravitation, as explained by Newton, is good, but grander when we find chemistry only an extension of the law of masses into particles, and that the atomic theory shows the action of chemistry to be mechanical also.

Metaphysics shows us a sort of gravitation operative also in the mental phenomena; and the terrible tabulation of the French statists brings every piece of whim and humour to be reducible also to exact numerical ratios. If one man in twenty thousand, or in thirty thousand, eats shoes or marries his grandmother, then in every twenty thousand or thirty thousand is found one man who eats shoes or marries his grandmother. What we call gravitation, and fancy ultimate, is one fork of a mightier stream for which we have yet no name.

Astronomy is excellent but it must come up into life to have its full value, and not remain there in globes and spaces. The globule of blood gyrates around its own axis in the human veins, as the planet

———

in the sky; and the circles of intellect relate to those of the heavens. Each law of nature has the like universality; eating, sleep or hybernation, rotation, generation, metamorphosis, vortical motion, which is seen in eggs as in planets. These grand rhymes or returns in nature —the dear, best-known face startling us at every turn under a mask so unexpected that we think it the face of a stranger, and carrying up the semblance into divine forms—delighted the prophetic eye of Swedenborg; and he must be reckoned a leader in that revolution, which, by giving to science an idea, has given to an aimless accumulation of experiments, guidance and form and a beating heart.

I own with some regret that his printed works amount to about fifty stout octavos, his scientific works being about half of the whole number; and it appears that a mass of manuscript, still unedited, remains in the Royal Library at Stockholm. The scientific works have just now been translated into English, in an excellent edition.

Swedenborg printed these scientific books in the ten years from 1734 to 1744, and they remained from that time neglected; and now, after their century is complete, he has at last found a pupil in Mr Wilkinson, in London, a philosophic critic, with a co-equal vigour of understanding and imagination comparable only to Lord Bacon's, who has produced his master's buried books to the day, and transferred them, with every advantage, from their forgotten Latin into English, to go round the world in our commercial and conquering tongue.

This startling re-appearance of Swedenborg, after a hundred years in his pupil is not the least remarkable fact in his history. Aided it is

———

said by the munificence of Mr Clissold, and also by his literary skill, this piece of poetic justice is done. The admirable preliminary discourses with which Mr Wilkinson has enriched these volumes, throw all the contemporary philosophy of England into shade and leave me nothing to say on their proper grounds.

The *Animal Kingdom*[19] is a book of wonderful merits. It was written with the highest end—to put science and the soul, long estranged from each other, at one again. It was an anatomist's account of the human body, in the highest style of poetry. Nothing can exceed the bold and brilliant treatment of a subject usually so dry and repulsive. He saw nature 'wreathing through an everlasting spiral, with wheels that never dry, on axles that never creak,' and sometimes sought 'to uncover those secret recesses where nature is sitting at the fires in the depths of her laboratory'; whilst the picture comes recommended by the hard fidelity with which it is based on practical anatomy. It is remarkable that this sublime genius decides peremptorily for the analytic, against the synthetic method; and, in a book whose genius is a daring poetic synthesis, claims to confine himself to a rigid experience.

He knows, if he only, the flowing of nature, and how wise was that old answer of Amasis to him who bade him drink up the sea—'Yes, willingly, if you will stop the rivers that flow in'.[20] Few knew as much about nature and her subtle manners, or expressed more subtly her goings. He thought as large a demand is made on our faith by nature, as by miracles.

'He noted that in her proceeding from first principles through her several subordinations, there was no state through which she did not pass, as if her path lay through all things...

For as often as she betakes herself upward from visible phenomena, or, in other words, withdraws herself inward, she instantly as it were disappears, while no one knows what has become of her, or whither she is gone: so that it is necessary to take science as a guide in pursuing her steps.' [21]

The pursuing the inquiry under the light of an end or final cause gives wonderful animation, a sort of personality to the whole writing. This book announces his favourite dogmas. The ancient doctrine of Hippocrates, that the brain is a gland; and of Leucippus, that the atom may be known by the mass; or, in Plato, the macrocosm by the microcosm; and, in the verses of Lucretius;

Ossa videlicet e pauxillis atque minutis
Ossibus, sic et de pauxillis atque minutis
Visceribus viscus gigni, sanguenque creari
Sanguinis inter se multis coeuntibus guttis;
Ex aurique putat micis consistere posse
Aurum, et de terris terram concrescere parvis;
Ignibus ex igneis, humorem humoribus esse.   Lib. 1. 835

'The principle of all things, entrails made

Of smallest entrails; bone, of smallest bone;
Blood, of small sanguine drops reduced to one;
Gold, of small grains; earth, of small sands compacted;
Small drops to water, sparks to fire contracted'; [22]

and which Malpighi had summed in his maxim that 'Nature exists
entire in leasts' [23] is a favourite thought of Swedenborg.

'It is a constant law of the organic body that large, compound,
or visible forms exist and subsist from smaller, simpler and
ultimately from invisible forms, which act similarly to the
larger ones, but more perfectly and more universally; and the
least forms so perfectly and universally as to involve an idea
representative of their entire universe'. [24]

The unities of each organ are so many little organs, homogeneous
with their compound: the unities of the tongue are little tongues;
those of the stomach, little stomachs; those of the heart are little
hearts. This fruitful idea furnishes a key to every secret. What was too
small for the eye to detect was read by the aggregates; what was too
large, by the units. There is no end to his application of the thought;

'Hunger is an aggregate of very many little hungers or losses
of blood by the little veins all over the body'. [25]

It is a key to his theology also;

'Man is a kind of very minute heaven, corresponding to the world of spirits and to heaven. Every particular idea of man, and every affection, yea, every smallest part of his affection, is an image and effigy of him. A spirit may be known from only a single thought. God is the grand man'. [26]

| Part Five |

T he hardihood and thoroughness of his study of nature required a theory of forms also.

'Forms ascend in order from the lowest to the highest. The lowest form is angular, or the terrestrial and corporeal. The second and next higher form is the circular, which is also called the perpetual-angular, because the circumference of a circle is a perpetual angle. The form above this is the spiral, parent and measure of circular forms: its diameters are not rectilinear, but variously circular, and have a spherical surface for centre; therefore it is called the perpetual-circular. The form above this is the vortical, or perpetual-spiral: next, the perpetual-vortical, or celestial: last, the perpetual-celestial, or spiritual.' [27]

Was it strange that a genius so bold should take the last step also,

---

should conceive that he might attain the science of all sciences, to unlock the meaning of the world? In the first volume of the *Animal Kingdom*, he broaches the subject in a remarkable note:

'In our doctrine of Representations and Correspondences we shall treat of both these symbolical and typical resemblances and of the astonishing things which occur, I will not say in the living body only, but throughout nature, and which correspond so entirely to supreme and spiritual things that one would swear that the physical world was purely symbolical of the spiritual world; insomuch that if we choose to express any natural truth in physical and definite vocal terms, and to convert these terms only into the corresponding and spiritual terms, we shall by this means elicit a spiritual truth, or theological dogma, in place of the physical truth or precept: although no mortal would have predicted that anything of the kind could possibly arise by bare literal transposition; inasmuch as the one precept, considered separately from the other, appears to have absolutely no relation to it. I intend hereafter to communicate a number of examples of such correspondences, together with a vocabulary containing the terms of spiritual things, as well as of the physical things for which they are to be substituted. This symbolism pervades the living body.' [28]

The fact thus explicitly stated is implied in all poetry, in allegory, in fable, in the use of emblems and in the structure of language. Plato knew it, as is evident from his twice bisected line in the sixth book of the *Republic*.[29] Lord Bacon had found that truth and nature differed only as seal and print; and he instanced some physical propositions with their translation into a moral or political sense. Behmen, and all mystics, imply this law in their dark riddle-writing. The poets, in as far as they are poets, use it but it is known to them only as the magnet was known for ages, as a toy.

Swedenborg first put the fact into a detached and scientific statement, because it was habitually present to him, and never not seen. It was involved, as we explained already, in the doctrine of identity and iteration because the mental series exactly tallies with the material series. It required an insight that could rank things in order and series; or rather it required such rightness of position that the poles of the eye should coincide with the axis of the world. The earth had fed its mankind through five or six millenniums, and they had sciences, religions, philosophies, and yet had failed to see the correspondence of meaning between every part and every other part. And, down to this hour, literature has no book in which the symbolism of things is scientifically opened.

One would say that as soon as men had the first hint that every sensible object—animal, rock, river, air—nay, space and time subsists not for itself, nor finally to a material end, but as a picture-language to tell another story of beings and duties, other science would be put by, and a science of such grand presage would absorb all faculties: that each man would ask of all objects what they mean:

Why does the horizon hold me fast with my joy and grief in this centre? Why hear I the same sense from countless differing voices, and read one never quite expressed fact in endless picture-language?——Yet whether it be that these things will not be intellectually learned, or that many centuries must elaborate and compose so rare and opulent a soul——there is no comet, rock-stratum, fossil, fish, quadruped, spider, or fungus, that, for itself, does not interest more scholars and classifiers than the meaning and upshot of the frame of things.

But Swedenborg was not content with the culinary use of the world. In his fifty-fourth year these thoughts held him fast and his profound mind admitted the perilous opinion, too frequent in religious history, that he was an abnormal person, to whom was granted the privilege of conversing with angels and spirits; and this ecstasy connected itself with just this office of explaining the moral import of the sensible world.

To a right perception, at once broad and minute, of the order of nature, he added the comprehension of the moral laws in their widest social aspects; but whatever he saw, through some excessive determination to form in his constitution, he saw not abstractly, but in pictures, heard it in dialogues, constructed it in events. When he attempted to announce the law most sanely, he was forced to couch it in parable.

Modern psychology offers no similar example of a deranged balance. The principal powers continued to maintain a healthy action and to a reader who can make due allowance in the report for the reporter's peculiarities, the results are still instructive, and a more striking

---

testimony to the sublime laws he announced than any that balanced dullness could afford. He attempts to give some account of the *modus* of the new state, affirming that 'his presence in the spiritual world is attended with a certain separation, but only as to the intellectual part of his mind, not as to the will part';[30] and he affirms that 'he sees with the internal sight the things that are in another life more clearly than he sees the things which are here in the world.' [31]

Having adopted the belief that certain books of the *Old* and *New Testaments* were exact allegories, or written in the angelic and ecstatic mode, he employed his remaining years in extricating from the literal, the universal sense. He had borrowed from Plato the fine fable of 'a most ancient people, men better than we and dwelling nigher to the gods';[32] and Swedenborg added that they used the earth symbolically; that these, when they saw terrestrial objects, did not think at all about them, but only about those which they signified.

The correspondence between thoughts and things henceforward occupied him, 'The very organic form resembles the end inscribed on it'.[33] A man is in general and in particular an organised justice or injustice, selfishness or gratitude. And the cause of this harmony he assigned in the *Arcana Calestia*.[34] 'The reason why all and single things, in the heavens and on earth, are representative, is because they exist from an influx of the Lord, through heaven'.[35] This design of exhibiting such correspondences, which, if adequately executed, would be the poem of the world, in which all history and science would play an essential part, was narrowed and defeated by the exclusively theologic direction which his inquiries took. His perception of nature is not human and universal, but is mystical and Hebraic.

He fastens each natural object to a theologic notion; a horse signifies carnal understanding; a tree, perception; the moon, faith; a cat means this; an ostrich that; an artichoke this other; and poorly tethers every symbol to a several ecclesiastic sense. The slippery Proteus is not so easily caught. In nature, each individual symbol plays innumerable parts, as each particle of matter circulates in turn through every system.

The central identity enables any one symbol to express successively all the qualities and shades of real being. In the transmission of the heavenly waters, every hose fits every hydrant. Nature avenges herself speedily on the hard pedantry that would chain her waves. She is no literalist. Everything must be taken genially, and we must be at the top of our condition to understand anything rightly.

His theological bias thus fatally narrowed his interpretation of nature, and the dictionary of symbols is yet to be written. But the interpreter whom mankind must still expect will find no predecessor who has approached so near to the true problem.

Part Six

S wedenborg styles himself in the title page of his books
'Servant of the Lord Jesus Christ'; and by force of intellect, and in effect, he is the last Father in the Church, and
is not likely to have a successor.

No wonder that his depth of ethical wisdom should give him influence as a teacher. To the withered traditional church yielding dry
catechisms he let in nature again and the worshipper escaping from
the vestry of verbs and texts is surprised to find himself a party to the
whole of his religion.

His religion thinks for him and is of universal application. He turns
it on every side; it fits every part of life, interprets and dignifies every
circumstance. Instead of a religion which visited him diplomatically
three or four times—when he was born, when he married, when he
fell sick and when he died, and for the rest never interfered with him—
here was a teaching which accompanied him all day, accompanied

him even into sleep and dreams; into his thinking, and showed him through what a long ancestry his thoughts descend; into society, and showed by what affinities he was girt to his equals and his counterparts; into natural objects, and showed their origin and meaning, what are friendly and what are hurtful; and opened the future world by indicating the continuity of the same laws. His disciples allege that their intellect is invigorated by the study of his books.

There is no such problem for criticism as his theological writings, their merits are so commanding, yet such grave deductions must be made. Their immense and sandy diffuseness is like the prairie or the desert, and their incongruities are like the last deliration. He is superfluously explanatory, and his feeling of the ignorance of men strangely exaggerated.

Men take truths of this nature very fast. Yet he abounds in assertions, he is a rich discoverer, and of things which most import us to know. His thought dwells in essential resemblances, like the resemblance of a house to the man who built it. He saw things in their law, in likeness of function, not of structure. There is an invariable method and order in his delivery of his truth, the habitual proceeding of the mind from inmost to outmost. What earnestness and weightiness, his eye never roving without one swell of vanity, or one look to self in any common form of literary pride! A theoretic or speculative man but whom no practical man in the universe could affect to scorn.

Plato is a gownsman: his garment, though of purple, and almost sky-woven, is an academic robe and hinders action with its voluminous folds. But this mystic is awful to Caesar. Lycurgus himself would bow.

The moral insight of Swedenborg, the correction of popular errors, the announcement of ethical laws, take him out of comparison with any other modern writer and entitle him to a place, vacant for some ages among the lawgivers of mankind. That slow but commanding influence which he has acquired, like that of other religious geniuses, must be excessive also, and have its tides, before it subsides into a permanent amount.

Of course what is real and universal cannot be confined to the circle of those who sympathise strictly with his genius, but will pass forth into the common stock of wise and just thinking. The world has a sure chemistry, by which it extracts what is excellent in its children and lets fall the infirmities and limitations of the grandest mind.

That metempsychosis which is familiar in the old mythology of the Greeks, collected in Ovid and in the Indian Transmigration, and is there *objective*, or really takes place in bodies by alien will—in Swedenborg's mind has a more philosophic character. It is subjective, or depends entirely upon the thought of the person. All things in the universe arrange themselves to each person anew, according to his ruling love.

Man is such as his affection and thought are. Man is man by virtue of willing, not by virtue of knowing and understanding. As he is, so he sees. The marriages of the world are broken up. Interiors associate all in the spiritual world. Whatever the angels looked upon was to them celestial. Each Satan appears to himself a man; to those as bad as he, a comely man; to the purified, a heap of carrion. Nothing can resist states: everything gravitates: like will to like: what we call poetic justice takes effect on the spot. We have come into a world which is a living poem. Everything is as I am. Bird and beast is not bird and beast, but emanation and effluvia of the minds and wills of men there present.

Every one makes his own house and state. The ghosts are tormented with the fear of death and cannot remember that they have died. They who are in evil and falsehood are afraid of all others. Such as have deprived themselves of charity, wander and flee: the societies which they approach discover their quality and drive them away. The covetous seem to themselves to be abiding in cells where their money is deposited, and these to be infested with mice. They who place merit in good works seem to themselves to cut wood. 'I asked such if they were not wearied? They replied, that they have not yet done work enough to merit heaven'.[36]

He delivers golden sayings which express with singular beauty the ethical laws; as when he uttered that famed sentence, that 'In heaven the angels are advancing continually to the springtime of their youth, so that the oldest angel appears the youngest':[37] 'The more angels, the more room';[38] 'The perfection of man is the love of use';[39] 'Man in his perfect form, is heaven';[40] 'What is from Him, is Him';[41] 'Ends always ascend as nature descends'.[42]

And the truly poetic account of the writing in the inmost heaven, which, as it consists of inflexions according to the form of heaven,

———

can be read without instruction. He almost justifies his claim to preter-
natural vision, by strange insights of the structure of the human
body and mind. 'It is never permitted to anyone in heaven to stand
behind another and look at the back of his head; for then the influx
which is from the Lord is disturbed'.[43]

The angels, from the sound of the voice, know a man's love; from
the articulation of the sound, his wisdom; and from the sense of the
words, his science.

———

| Part Seven |

I n the *Conjugial Love*, he has unfolded the science of marriage. Of this book one would say that with the highest
elements it has failed of success. It came near to be the
Hymn of Love, which Plato attempted in the 'Banquet'; the love, which,
Dante says, Casella sang[44] among the angels in Paradise; and which,
as rightly celebrated, in its genesis, fruition and effect, might well
entrance the souls, as it would lay open the genesis of all institutions,
customs and manners.

The book had been grand if the Hebraism had been omitted and
the law stated without Gothicism, as ethics, and with that scope for
ascension of state which the nature of things requires. It is a fine
Platonic development of the science of marriage; teaching that sex is
universal, and not local; virility in the male qualifying every organ,
act, and thought; and the feminine in woman. Therefore in the real
or spiritual world the nuptial union is not momentary, but incessant

---

and total; and chastity not a local, but a universal virtue; unchastity being discovered as much in the trading, or planting, or speaking, or philosophising, as in generation; and that, though the virgins he saw in heaven were beautiful, the wives were incomparably more beautiful, and went on increasing in beauty evermore.

Yet Swedenborg, after his mode, pinned his theory to a temporary form. He exaggerates the circumstance of marriage and, though he finds false marriages on earth, fancies a wiser choice in heaven. But of progressive souls, all loves and friendships are momentary. *Do you love me?* means, Do you see the same truth? If you do, we are happy with the same happiness: but presently one of us passes into the perception of new truth, we are divorced, and no tension in nature can hold us to each other. I know how delicious is this cup of love— I existing for you, you existing for me; but it is a child's clinging to his toy; an attempt to eternise the fireside and nuptial chamber; to keep the picture-alphabet through which our first lessons are prettily conveyed.

The Eden of God is bare and grand: like the outdoor landscape remembered from the evening fireside, it seems cold and desolate whilst you cower over the coals, but once abroad again, we pity those who can forego the magnificence of nature for candle-light and cards. Perhaps the true subject of the *Conjugial Love* is Conversation whose laws are profoundly eliminated. It is false, if literally applied to marriage. For God is the bride or bridegroom of the soul. Heaven is not the pairing of two, but the communion of all souls. We meet and

———

dwell an instant under the temple of one thought and part as though we parted not, to join another thought in other fellowships of joy.

So far from there being anything divine in the low and proprietary sense of *Do you love me*? it is only when you leave and lose me by casting yourself on a sentiment which is higher than both of us, that I draw near and find myself at your side; and I am repelled if you fix your eye on me and demand love. In fact, in the spiritual world, we change sexes every moment. You love the worth in me; then I am your husband: but it is not me, but the worth, that fixes the love; and that worth is a drop of the ocean of worth that is beyond me. Meantime I adore the greater worth in another, and so become his wife. He aspires to a higher worth in another spirit, and is wife or receiver of that influence.

Whether from a self-inquisitorial habit that he grew into from jealousy of the sins to which men of thought are liable, he has acquired in disentangling and demonstrating that particular form of moral disease, an acumen which no conscience can resist. I refer to his feeling of the profanation of thinking to what is good, 'from scientifics'. 'To reason about faith, is to doubt and deny'.[45] He was painfully alive to the difference between knowing and doing, and this sensibility is incessantly expressed. Philosophers are, therefore, vipers, cockatrices, asps, hemorrhoids, presters, and flying serpents; literary men are conjurors and charlatans.

But this topic suggests a sad afterthought, that here we find the seat of his own pain.

———

———

Possibly Swedenborg paid the penalty of introverted faculties. Success, or a fortunate genius, seems to depend on a happy adjustment of heart and brain; on a due proportion hard to hit of moral and mental power, which perhaps obeys the law of those chemical ratios which make a proportion in volumes necessary to combination, as when gases will combine in certain fixed rates, but not at any rate. It is hard to carry a full cup; and this man, profusely endowed in heart and mind, early fell into dangerous discord with himself.

In his *Animal Kingdom* he surprised us by declaring that he loved analysis, and not synthesis; and now, after his fiftieth year, he falls into jealousy of his intellect; and though aware that truth is not solitary nor is goodness solitary, but both must ever mix and marry, he makes war on his mind, takes the part of the conscience against it, and, on all occasions, traduces and blasphemes it. The violence is instantly avenged. Beauty is disgraced, love is unlovely, when truth, the half part of heaven is denied as much as when a bitterness in men of talent leads to satire and destroys the judgment.

He is wise, but wise in his own despite. There is an air of infinite grief and the sound of wailing all over and through this lurid universe. A vampire sits in the seat of the prophet and turns with gloomy appetite to the images of pain. Indeed, a bird does not more readily weave its nest, or a mole bore into the ground, than this seer of the souls substructs a new hell and pit, each more abominable than the last, round every new crew of offenders.

He was let down through a column that seemed of brass but it was

———

formed of angelic spirits that he might descend safely amongst the unhappy and witness the vastation of souls and heard there, for a long continuance, and their lamentations: he saw their tormentors, who increase and strain pangs to infinity; he saw the hell of the jugglers, the hell of the assassins, the hell of the lascivious; the hell of robbers, who kill and boil men; the infernal tun of the deceitful; the excrementitious hells; the hell of the revengeful, whose faces resembled a round, broad cake, and their arms rotate like a wheel. Except Rabelais and Dean Swift nobody ever had such science of filth and corruption.

| Part Eight |

T hese books should be used with caution. It is dangerous to sculpture these evanescing images of thought. True in transition, they become false if fixed. It requires for his just apprehension almost a genius equal to his own. But when his visions become the stereotyped language of multitudes of persons of all degrees of age and capacity, they are perverted.

The wise people of the Greek race were accustomed to lead the most intelligent and virtuous young men, as part of their education, through the Eleusinian Mysteries, wherein, with much pomp and graduation, the highest truths known to ancient wisdom were taught. An ardent and contemplative young man, at eighteen or twenty years, might read once these books of Swedenborg, these mysteries of love and conscience, and then throw them aside forever. Genius is ever haunted by similar dreams, when the hells and the heavens are opened to it. But these pictures are to be held as mystical, that is, as a quite arbitrary and accidental picture of the truth—not as the truth. Any other symbol would be as good: then this is safely seen.

Swedenborg's system of the world wants central spontaneity; it is dynamic not vital and lacks power to generate life. There is no individual in it. The Universe is a gigantic crystal, all whose atoms and laminae lie in uninterrupted order and with unbroken unity, but cold and still. What seems an individual and a will, is none.

There is an immense chain of intermediation, extending from centre to extremes, which bereaves every agency of all freedom and character. The universe in his poem suffers under a magnetic sleep, and only reflects the mind of the magnetiser. Every thought comes into each mind by influence from a society of spirits that surround it, and into these from a higher society, and so on.

All his types mean the same few things. All his figures speak one speech. All his interlocutors Swedenborgise. Be they who they may, to this complexion must they come at last. This Charon ferries them all over in his boat; kings, counsellors, cavaliers, doctors, Sir Isaac Newton, Sir Hans Sloane, King George II, Mahomet, or whomsoever, and all gather one grimness of hue and style.

Only when Cicero comes by, our gentle seer sticks a little at saying he talked with Cicero, and with a touch of human relenting remarks, 'one whom it was given me to believe was Cicero';[46] and when the *soi disant* Roman opens his mouth, Rome and eloquence have ebbed away—it is plain theologic Swedenborg like the rest. His heavens and hells are dull; fault of want of individualism. The thousandfold relation of men is not there.

The interest that attaches in nature to each man because he is right by his wrong and wrong by his right; because he defies all dogmatising and classification, so many allowances and contingencies and futurities are to be taken into account, strong by his vices, often paralysed by his virtues—sinks into entire sympathy with his society. This want reacts to the centre of the system. Though the agency of 'the Lord' is in every line referred to by name, it never becomes alive. There is no lustre in that eye which gazes from the centre, and which should vivify the immense dependency of beings.

The vice of Swedenborg's mind is its theological determination. Nothing with him has the liberality of universal wisdom, but we are always in a church. That Hebrew muse which taught the lore of right and wrong to men had the same excess of influence for him it has had for the nations. The mode as well as the essence, was sacred.

Palestine is ever the more valuable as a chapter in universal history, and ever the less an available element in education. The genius of Swedenborg, largest of all modern souls in this department of thought, wasted itself in the endeavour to reanimate and conserve what had already arrived at its natural term, and, in the great secular Providence, was retiring from its prominence, before western modes of thought and expression. Swedenborg and Behmen both failed by attaching themselves to the Christian symbol, instead of to the moral sentiment, which carries innumerable christianities, humanities, divinities in its bosom.

The excess of influence shows itself in the incongruous importation of a foreign rhetoric. 'What have I to do,' asks the impatient reader, 'with jasper and sardonyx, beryl and chalcedony; what with arks and passovers, ephahs and ephods; what with lepers and emerods; what with heave offerings and unleavened bread, chariots of fire, dragons crowned and horned, behemoth and unicorn? Good for Orientals these are nothing to me. The more learning you bring to explain them, the more glaring the impertinence. The more coherent and elaborate the system, the less I like it. I say, with the Spartan, "Why do you speak so much to the purpose, of that which is nothing to the purpose?"[47] My learning is such as God gave me in my birth and habit, in the delight and study of my eyes and not of another man's. Of all absurdities, this of some foreigner proposing to take away my rhetoric and substitute his own, and amuse me with pelican and stork, instead of thrush and robin; palm-trees and shittim-wood, instead of sassafras and hickory—seems the most needless'.

Locke said, 'God, when he makes the prophet, does not unmake the man'.[48] Swedenborg's history points the remark. The parish disputes in the Swedish Church between the friends and foes of Luther and Melancthon, concerning 'faith alone' and 'works alone' intrude themselves into his speculations upon the economy of the universe, and of the celestial societies. The Lutheran bishop's son, for whom the heavens are opened, so that he sees with eyes and in the richest symbolic forms the awful truth of things, and utters again in his books, as under a heavenly mandate, the indisputable secrets of moral nature—with all these grandeurs resting upon him, remains the Lutheran bishop's son; his judgments are those of a Swedish polemic, and his vast enlargements purchased by adamantine limitations.

He carries his controversial memory with him in his visits to the souls. He is like Michaelangelo, who, in his frescoes, put the cardinal who had offended him to roast under a mountain of devils; or like Dante who avenged in vindictive melodies all his private wrongs; or perhaps still more like Montaigne's parish priest who, if a hail-storm passes over the village, thinks the day of doom is come and the cannibals already have got the pip. Swedenborg confounds us not less with the pains of Melancthon and Luther and Wolfius, and his own books, which he advertises among the angels.

| Part Nine |

U nder the same theologic cramp, many of his dogmas are bound. His cardinal position in morals is that evils should be shunned as sins. But he does not know what evil is, or what good is, who thinks any ground remains to be occupied, after saying that evil is to be shunned as evil. I doubt not he was led by the desire to insert the element of personality of Deity. But nothing is added.

One man, you say, dreads erysipelas—show him that this dread is evil; or one dreads hell; show him that *dread* is evil. He who loves goodness harbours angels, reveres reverence and lives with God. The less we have to do with our sins the better. No man can afford to waste his moments in compunctions. 'That is active duty', say the Hindus, 'which is not for our bondage; that is knowledge, which is for our liberation: all other duty is good only unto weariness'.[49]

Another dogma growing out of this pernicious theologic limitation is his Inferno. Swedenborg has devils. Evil, according to old philosophers, is good in the making. That pure malignity can exist is the extreme proposition of unbelief. It is not to be entertained by a rational agent; it is atheism, it is the last profanation. Euripides rightly said;

'Goodness and being in the gods are one;
He who imputes ill to them makes them none'.[50]

To what a painful perversion had Gothic theology arrived that Swedenborg admitted no conversion for evil spirits! But the Divine effort is never relaxed; the carrion in the sun will convert itself to grass and flowers; and man, though in brothels, or jails, or on gibbets, is on his way to all that is good and true. Burns, with the wild humour of his apostrophe to poor 'auld Nickie Ben', 'O wad ye tak a thought and mend!',[51] has the advantage of the vindictive theologian.

Everything is superficial and perishes but love and truth only. The largest is always the truest sentiment, and we feel the more generous spirit of the Indian Vishnu;

'I am the same to all mankind. There is not one who is worthy of my love or hatred. They who serve me with adoration—I am in them, and they in me. If one whose ways are altogether evil serve me alone, he is as respectable as the just man; he is altogether well employed; he soon becometh of a virtuous spirit and obtaineth eternal happiness.'[52]

For the anomalous pretension of Revelations of the other world only his probity and genius can entitle it to any serious regard. His revelations destroy their credit by running into detail.

If a man say that the Holy Ghost has informed him that the Last Judgment (or the last of the judgments) took place in 1757; or that the Dutch in the other world live in a heaven by themselves, and the English in a heaven by themselves; I reply that the Spirit which is holy is reserved, taciturn, and deals in laws.

The rumours of ghosts and hobgoblins gossip and tell fortunes. The teachings of the high Spirit are abstemious, and, in regard to particulars, negative. Socrates's Genius did not advise him to act or to find, but if he purposed to do somewhat not advantageous, it dissuaded him. 'What God is,' he said, 'I know not; what he is not, I know'.[53] The Hindus have denominated the Supreme Being, the 'Internal Check.'[54]

The illuminated Quakers explained their Light, not as somewhat which leads to any action, but it appears as an obstruction to any thing unfit. But the right examples are private experiences, which are absolutely at one on this point. Strictly speaking, Swedenborg's revelation is a confounding of planes—a capital offence in so learned a categorist. This is to carry the law of surface into the plane of substance, to carry individualism and its fopperies into the realm of essences and generals—which is dislocation and chaos.

The secret of heaven is kept from age to age. No imprudent, no sociable angel ever dropped an early syllable to answer the longings of saints, the fears of mortals. We should have listened on our knees to any favourite who by stricter obedience had brought his thoughts into parallelism with the celestial currents and could hint to human ears the scenery and circumstance of the newly parted soul. But it is certain that it must tally with what is best in nature. It must not be inferior in tone to the already known works of the artist who sculptures the globes of the firmament and writes the moral law. It must be fresher than rainbows, stabler than mountains, agreeing with flowers, with tides and the rising and setting of autumnal stars. Melodious poets shall be hoarse as street ballads when once the penetrating key-note of nature and spirit is sounded, the earthbeat, seabeat, heartbeat, which makes the tune to which the sun rolls, and the globule of blood, and the sap of trees.

In this mood we hear the rumour that the seer has arrived, and his tale is told. But there is no beauty, no heaven: for angels, goblins. The sad muse loves night and death and the pit. His Inferno is mesmeric. His spiritual world bears the same relation to the generosities and joys of truth of which human souls have already made us cognisant, as a man's bad dreams bear to his ideal life. It is indeed very like, in its endless power of lurid pictures, to the phenomena of dreaming, which nightly turns many an honest gentleman, benevolent but dyspeptic, into a wretch, skulking like a dog about the outer yards and kennels of creation.

When he mounts into the heaven, I do not hear its language. A man should not tell me that he has walked among the angels; his proof is that his eloquence makes me one. Shall the archangels be less majestic and sweet than the figures that have actually walked the earth?

These angels that Swedenborg paints give us no very high idea of their discipline and culture: they are all country parsons: their heaven is a *fête champêtre*, an evangelical picnic, or French distribution of prizes to virtuous peasants. Strange, scholastic, didactic, passionless, bloodless man, who denotes classes of souls as a botanist disposes of a carex, and visits doleful hells as a stratum of chalk or hornblende! He has no sympathy. He goes up and down the world of men, a modern Rhadamanthus in goldheaded cane and peruke, and with nonchalance and the air of a referee, distributes souls.

The warm, many-weathered, passionate-peopled world is to him a grammar of hieroglyphs or an emblematic freemason's procession. How different is Jacob Behmen! *he* is tremulous with emotion and listens awestruck, with the gentlest humanity, to the Teacher whose lessons he conveys; and when he asserts that, 'in some sort, love is greater than God', [55] his heart beats so high that the thumping against his leathern coat is audible across the centuries. 'Tis a great difference.

Behmen is healthily and beautifully wise, notwithstanding the mystical narrowness and incommunicableness. Swedenborg is disagreeably wise, and with all his accumulated gifts, paralyses and repels.

It is the best sign of a great nature that it opens a foreground and like the breath of morning landscapes invites us onward. Swedenborg is retrospective, nor can we divest him of his mattock and shroud. Some minds are forever restrained from descending into nature; others are forever prevented from ascending out of it. With a force of many men he could never break the umbilical cord which held him to nature and he did not rise to the platform of pure genius.

It is remarkable that this man, who, by his perception of symbols, saw the poetic construction of things and the primary relation of mind to matter, remained entirely devoid of the whole apparatus of poetic expression, which that perception creates.

He knew the grammar and rudiments of the *mother tongue*— how could he not read off one strain into music? Was he like Saadi, who, in his vision, designed to fill his lap with the celestial flowers as presents for his friends; but the fragrance of the roses so intoxicated him that the skirt dropped from his hands? or is reporting a breach of the manners of that heavenly society? or was it that he saw the vision intellectually, and hence that chiding of the intellectual that pervades his books?

Be it as it may, his books have no melody, no emotion, no humour, no relief to the dead prosaic level. In his profuse and accurate imagery is no pleasure, for there is no beauty. We wander forlorn in a lack-lustre landscape. No bird ever sang in all these gardens of the dead. The entire want of poetry in so transcendent a mind betokens the disease and like a hoarse voice in a beautiful person is a kind of warning.

I think, sometimes, he will not be read longer. His great name will turn a sentence. His books have become a monument. His laurel so largely mixed with cypress, a charnelbreath so mingles with the temple incense, that boys and maids will shun the spot.

———

Yet in this immolation of genius and fame at the shrine of conscience, is a merit sublime beyond praise. He lived to purpose: he
gave a verdict. He elected goodness as the clue to which the soul
must cling in all this labyrinth of nature. Many opinions conflict as
to the true centre. In the shipwreck, some cling to running rigging,
some to cask and barrel, some to spars, some to mast; the pilot chooses
with science—I plant myself here, all will sink before this, 'he comes
to land who sails with me'.[56]

Do not rely on heavenly favour, or on compassion to folly, or on
prudence, on common sense, the old usage and main chance of men:
nothing can keep you—not fate, nor health, nor admirable intellect;
none can keep you, but rectitude only, rectitude forever and ever!
And with a tenacity that never swerved in all his studies, inventions,
dreams, he adheres to this brave choice. I think of him as of some
transmigrating votary of Indian legend, who says though I be dog,
or jackal, or pismire, in the last rudiments of nature, under what
integument or ferocity, I cleave to right, as the sure ladder that leads
up to man and to God.

Swedenborg has rendered a double service to mankind, which is
now only beginning to be known. By the science of experiment and
use he made his first steps: he observed and published the laws of
nature; and ascending by just degrees from events to their summits
and causes he was fired with piety at the harmonies he felt and
abandoned himself to his joy and worship. This was his first service.
If the glory was too bright for his eyes to bear, if he staggered under

the trance of delight, the more excellent is the spectacle he saw, the realities of being which beam and blaze through him, and which no infirmities of the prophet are suffered to obscure; and he renders a second passive service to men, not less than the first, perhaps in the great circle of being—and, in the retributions of spiritual nature, not less glorious or less beautiful to himself.

Notes
Glossary
Index

| Notes |

[1] This is a modification of a passage from *Practical Philosophy of the Muhammadan People, Exhibited in Its Professed Connexion with the European, so far as to Render Either an Introduction to the Other; Being a Translation of the Akhlak-i-Jalaly, the Most Esteemed Ethical Work of Middle Asia, from the Persian of Fakir Jany Muhammad Asäad* (trans. W F Thompson; London, 1839), page 12: 'God saith, *The heavens, the earth, and all that is between them, we created not in sport;* - and again he saith, *Then think ye we have created ye in jest, and that ye are not to return to us?*' Emerson identified two verses from the Koran in this quotation: 21.16 and 23.115.

[2] *ibid.* page 114.

[3] *ibid.* page 391. For both this and the preceding note, 'Persian' refers to Emerson's source in general—in which the verse is unattributed—and not a specific poet.

[4] *ibid.* p. 25.

[5] *The Vishnu Purana*, p. 650 (bk. VI, ch. vii). Edition most likely used by Emerson: H H Wilson. London, 1840.

[6] *Meno.* Plato. 81 C-D in *The Works of Plato* (trans. Thomas Taylor and Floyer Sydenham, London: Wiks, 1804).

---

[7] *Select Works of Plotinus* (trans. Thomas Taylor; London, 1817), p. 506 (*Ennead* VI, bk. 9, para. xi).

[8] *Absalom and Achitophel*. Dryden. Part I, line 158.

[9] *Hamlet*. William Shakespeare. I, iv: 20-22.

[10] *Daedalus Hyperboreus (The Northern Inventor)*. Scientific journal first published by Swedenborg in 1716-18.

[11] *The Principia; or, The First Principles of Natural Things, Being New Attempts toward a Philosophical Explanation of the Elementary World (Principia Rerum Naturalium)*. Emanuel Swedenborg. 1734. English edition translated by Augustus Clissold in 2 vols., London and Boston, and published in 1845-6. Current edition is the 1988 re-print by The Swedenborg Scientific Association.

[12] *Principia (Philosophiae Naturalis Principia Mathematica)*. Isaac Newton, 1687. Swedenborg was born in January, 1688.

[13] Attributed to Malpighi. Translated as 'Nature exists entire in leasts'.

[14] A translation of 'Natura sibi semper est similis' attributed to Linnaeus in *The Journals and Miscellaneous Notebooks of Ralph Waldo Emerson* (Edited by William H Gilman et al. 16 vols., The Belknap Press of Harvard University Press, 1960-1982), XII, 555, 556, but attributed to Malpighi in *The Complete Works of Ralph Waldo Emerson*. Edited by Edward Waldo Emerson. 12 vols., Boston and New York: Houghton, Mifflin and Company, 1903-04, IV, 326.

[15] *The Economy of the Animal Kingdom*. Emanuel Swedenborg. 1740-42. English edition translated by Augustus Clissold. Current edition is the 1955 re-print by the Swedenborg Scientific Association.

[16] *The Principia*. Emanuel Swedenborg. 1734. (trans. Augustus Clissold), pt. I, ch. I, sec. 4.

[17] Translation of 'Natura sibi semper est similis'. See note 14.

[18] *Timaeus*. Plato. Written sometime during 360-348 BC. Current English edition translated by Desmond Prichard Lee, Penguin Classics, 1971.

[19] *The Animal Kingdom*. Emanuel Swedenborg. 1744. English edition

translated by J J G Wilkinson in 1843. Current edition is the 1960 re-print by the Swedenborg Scientific Association.

[20] This story is found in Plutarch's *Moralia*, 151 B-D. Emerson most likely recalled it from 'The Banquet of the Seven Wise Men' in *Plutarch's Morals: translated from the Greek by several hands* (trans. M Morgan, S Ford, W Dillingham, T Hoy and others, 5 vols., London, 1718), II, 11.

[21] The source of this quotation has not been found.

[22] *De Rerum Natura*. Lucretius. Lib. 1, 835-41. The English translation of the Latin quotation is from Thomas Stanley, *The History of Philosophy* (4th edition, London: A Millar, 1743), pt. II, 'Anaxagoras,' ch. I, sec. 1.

[23] See note 13.

[24] This is a paraphrase from Swedenborg's *The Animal Kingdom* (trans. Wilkinson), vol. 1, ch. iv, p. 129.

[25] *ibid.*

[26] Emerson seems to be paraphrasing several important tenets of Swedenborg's theology from various works including *Arcana Caelestia* (see note 34 below), *Divine Love and Wisdom* (1763, current English edition: The Swedenborg Society, 1987, trans. Clifford and Doris Harley), and *Divine Providence* (1764, current English edition: The Swedenborg Society, 1988, trans. Dick and Pulsford).

[27] This is a paraphrase from Swedenborg's *The Animal Kingdom* (trans. Wilkinson), vol. 1, ch. iv, sec. 97, footnote (*f*), p. 126.

[28] *ibid.*, vol. 1, ch. xiv, sec. 293, footnote (*u*).

[29] *Republic*. Plato. Written sometime during 388-367 BC. Current English edition translated by Desmond Prichard Lee, Penguin Classics, 2003. For Plato's 'twice bisected line' see *Republic*, 509D-510C, 511D-E (bk VI, ch. 20, 21). For Emerson's discussion of this see his essay 'Plato, or the Philosopher'.

[30] *Emanuel Swedenborg*. J J G Wilkinson. Page 206. London: William Newsbury, 1849.

[31] This is a paraphrase from Swedenborg's *A Treatise Concerning Heaven*

and its Wonders and Hell §126, ch. XV. Current English edition published as *Heaven and Hell*: The Swedenborg Society, 1992, (trans. D Harley).

[32] *Philebus*. Plato. 16 C.

[33] This is a paraphrase of Swedenborg, *Arcana Caelestia* §4223, Gen., ch. xxxi.

[34] *Arcana Caelestia*. Emanuel Swedenborg. 1749-56. Current English edition translated by John Elliott, The Swedenborg Society, 1983-99.

[35] *Arcana Caelestia* §1807, Gen., ch. xv.

[36] *Arcana Caelestia* §391, Gen.,ch. iv; §938, ch. vii; §1110, ch. ix (repeated at §4943, ch. xxxviii).

[37] Probably expanded from Swedenborg's *Conjugial Love* §44, or *Arcana Caelestia* §553, Gen., ch. vi or *A Treatise Concerning Heaven and...Hell* §414, ch. XLII.

[38] Probably derived from *ibid.*, ch. IX, §71.

[39] *Conjugial Love* §183. Emanuel Swedenborg. Current English edition translated by Dr John Chadwick. The Swedenborg Society, 1996.

[40] *A Treatise Concerning Heaven and...Hell*. Emanuel Swedenborg, §60, ch. VIII,.

[41] *ibid.*, §§260-1, ch. XXIX.

[42] The source of this quotation has not been found.

[43] *A Treatise Concerning Heaven and...Hell*. Emanuel Swedenborg, §144, ch. XVI,.

[44] See *Purgatorio*. Dante. II, 76-117.

[45] *Arcana Caelestia*. Emanuel Swedenborg. §§229-233, Gen., ch. iii.

[46] *A Treatise Concerning Heaven and...Hell*. Emanuel Swedenborg. §322, ch. XXXVI.

[47] Adapted from Plutarch's *Lives* (trans. John and William Langhorne), 'Lycurgus,' para. xx.

[48] *An Essay Concerning Human Understanding*. John Locke. Bk. IV, ch. XIX, para. 14.

[49] *The Vishnu Purana*, p. 139 (bk. I, ch. xix).

[50] *Plutarch's Morals* (trans. M Morgan etc., 5 vols., London, 1718), II, 54.

[51] 'Address to the Deil'. R Burns. st. xxi.

[52] These words are spoken by Krishna (not Vishnu) in *The Bhagvat-Geeta, or Dialogues of Kreeshna and Arjoon* (trans. Charles Wilkins, London, 1785), pages 81-2 (ch. IX, 29-31).

[53] *The History of Philosophy*. Stanley. pt. III, 'Socrates,' ch. V, sec. 1.

[54] *Miscellaneous Essays*. Henry Thomas Colebrooke. 2 vols. (London, 1837), I, 341. Cf. Colebrooke's essay 'On the Philosophy of the Hindus: Part IV. On the Vedanta'.

[55] Emerson's rendering of the paradox in Jacob Behmen's *The Way to Christ*, (bk. VI, para. 26-27), taken from *The Works of Jacob Behmen*, (ed. G Ward and T Langcake, trans. Sparrow, Ellistone and Blunden, 4 vols., London: M Richardson, 1764-1781).

[56] From Nathaniel P Willis' poem entitled 'Lines on Leaving Europe'.

Glossary of names cited

Amasis (600-526 BC): Ahmose II Khnemibre, King of Egypt (ruled 570-526 BC).

Aristotle (384-322 BC): Along with Plato and Socrates, one of the key influences of western philosophy.

Bacon, Francis (1561-1626): Philosopher, lawyer and statesman. One of the fathers of modern thought.

Behmen, Jacob (1575-1624): German mystic, also known as Boehme.

Boerhaave, Hermann (1668-1738): Dutch physician and professor of medicine.

Brunswicks: The House of Brunswick (Brunswick is the English translation of the German Braunschweig). One of Swedenborg's patrons, Ludwig Rudolph of Braunschweig-Wolfenbuettel (1671-1735) was Duke of Brunswick (1731-5).

Bunyan, John (1628-88): Author of *The Pilgrim's Progress*, 1678-84.

Buonarrati, Michaelangelo (1475-1564): Italian sculptor, painter, architect and poet.

Burns, Robert (1759-96): Scottish poet.

Caesar, Gaius Julius (c. 102-44 BC): Roman statesman and general.

Casella: Dante's friend, the beautiful singer. Cf. *Purgatorio*, II, 76-117.

Charles XII (1682-1718): King of Sweden (1697-1718).

Charon: Figure from Greek mythology. Charon was a ferryman in the underworld who transported souls across the river Acheron to the kingdom of the dead.

Cicero, Marcus Tullius (106-43 BC): Roman orator, politician and philosopher.

Clissold, Augustus (1797-1882): Anglican clergyman, Swedenborgian scholar and translator of Swedenborg's *Principia* and *The Economy of the Animal Kingdom*.

Cristierns: This refers to the forenames (also spelled Christiern, Christian, Kristian) of a succession of Swedish, Scandanavian and Saxon kings and nobles who reigned during Swedenborg's lifetime.

Dante, Alighieri (1265-1321): Renowned Italian poet.

Descartes, René (1596-1650): French mathematician, scientist, and philosopher. The first modern philosopher to oppose scholastic Aristotelianism.

Euripides (485-406 BC): Greek tragic dramatist.

Eustachius, Bartolomeo (1524-74): Distinguished anatomist of the Renaissance period.

Fox, George (1624-1691): Founder of the Society of Friends (or Quakers).

Frederics: This refers to the forenames (also spelled Frederick) of several kings of Sweden, Norway and Denmark, and electors of Saxony who reigned during Swedenborg's lifetime.

George II (1683-1760): King of Great Britain and Ireland (1727-1760).

Gilbert, William (1544 -1603): Physician and pioneer of research into magnetism who became a distinguished man of science during the reign of Queen Elizabeth I.

Grotius, Hugo (1583-1645): Dutch jurist and a major contributor to international law.

Guyon, Jeanne-Marie Bouvier de La Motte (1648-1717): Also known as Madame Du Chesnoy Guyon, a French mystic and writer.

Harvey, William (1578-1657): English physician and discoverer of the circulation

---

of blood and of the function of the heart as a pump.

Heister, Lorenz (1683-1758): German surgeon and writer.

Hippocrates (460-377 BC): Greek physician.

Hopken, Count Anders Johan von (1712-89): Swedish statesman and prime minister (1751-62). Author and friend of Swedenborg.

Humboldt, Alexander von (1769-1859): German naturalist and explorer, a major figure in the field of physical geography and biogeography.

Khair, Abul (967-1049): Abu Said Abolkhair Abu Said Fazlollah Ibn Abolkhair was schooled in sciences, but became renowned as a mystic.

Leeuwenhoek, Antony Van (1632-1723): Dutch naturalist and anatomist who helped further microscopism.

Leibnitz, Gottfried Wilhelm (1646-1716): German philosopher, mathematician and political adviser.

Leucippus (c. 480-420 BC): Greek philosopher who, according to Aristotle, was the founder of Atomism.

Linnaeus, Carolus (1707-1778): Carl von Linné, Swedish botanist and explorer. The first to frame principles for defining genera and species of organisms.

Locke, John (1632-1704): Foremost English philosopher of the 17th century.

Lucretius (94?-55 BC): Titus Lucretius Carus, Roman poet. He set the atomic theory of Epicurus in hexameters in *De Rerum Natura*.

Luther, Martin (1483-1546): German priest, scholar and founder of the Protestant Reformation.

Lycurgus: Legendary founder of the Spartan constitution. The earliest mention of him is in Herodotus, and he is associated with the 7th century BC. However, little is known about him, not even if he was a real man, a god or a figure from mythology.

Mahomet (570-632 BC): Mohammed, prophet of Islam.

Malpighi, Marcello (1628-94): Italian physician and biologist who founded the science of microscopic anatomy.

Melancthon, Philip (1497-1560): German author, humanist, reformer, theologian and educator.

Menu (Manu): In Indian philosophy one of a class of Demiurges, the first of them being identified with Brahma. The laws of Manu (a section of the Vedas containing a code of civil and religious law) are ascribed to the seventh Manu, called Vaivasvata ('the sun-born').

Monro, Alexander (1733-1817): Trained in anatomy by his father and known as a gifted physician and teacher.

Montaigne, Michael de (1533-1592): French writer whose essays set a new standard for self-portrait.

Newton, Sir Isaac (1624-1727): A mathematician and theoretical physicist. Inventor of calculus and discoverer of the law of gravity.

Ovid (43 BC-17 AD): Publius Ovidius Naso. Classical poet whose works include *Metamorphoses* and *Amores*.

Pascal, Blaise (1623-1662): French mathematician, physicist and philosopher.

Plato (428-347 BC): Along with Socrates and Aristotle, one of the leading influences of western philosophy.

Plotinus (204-270): Author of the *Enneads* and the founder of Neo-Platonism.

Porphyry (232-c.305): Editor of Plotinus' writings and lectures. His simplification of Plotinus' thought is said to have influenced Macrobius and Augustine.

Proteus: A Greek mythological man of the sea, and shepherd of the sea's flock.

Rabelais, François (1494-1553): French writer and priest who was also a physician and humanist.

Rhadamanthus: Son of Zeus and Europa, according to Greek mythology.

Saadi or *Sa'di* (1184-1291): Persian Sufi poet, one of the greatest figures in classical Persian literature.

Schlichting, Jan Daniel (b.1703): Dutch embryologist.

Seena, Abu Ali (980-1037): Abu Ali al-Husain ibn Abdallah ibn Sina, also known by the Latin name Avicenna. Philosopher, physician, scientist and author of the famous *The Canon of Medicine*.

Selden, John (1584-1654): Legal antiquarian, Orientalist, politician and leading English historian.

Shakespeare, William (1564-1616): English playwright and poet.

Sloane, Sir Hans (1660-1753): Noted physician and scientist whose collections were the founding core of the British Museum and later the Natural History Museum.

Socrates (470-399 BC): Athenian philosopher whose *Dialogues* were recorded by Plato.

Swammerdam, Jan (1637-80): Dutch naturalist who was the first to observe and describe red blood cells.

Swift, Jonathan (1667-1745): Satirical writer famed for his novel, *Gulliver's Travels*. Swift became Dean of St. Patrick's Cathedral, Dublin in 1713.

Vesalius, Andreas (1514-1564): Renaissance Flemish physician who revolutionised the study of biology and the practice of medicine by his careful description of the anatomy of the human body.

Vishnu: Also known as Narayana, one of the gods of Hinduism.

Wilkinson, J J G (1812-99): Homeopathic doctor, social reformer, Swedenborgian scholar and translator. A friend of Emerson and Henry James senior.

Wilson, Alexander (1718-92): Scottish philosophical writer and physician.

Winslow, Jacob (1669-1760): Danish descriptive anatomist.

Wolff and *Wolfius, Christian* (1679-1754): Mathematician and philosopher. Influenced by Leibniz and Descartes and an important influence on German rationalist thought.

Index

Abu Ali Seena, 3
Abul Khair, 3
Amasis, 21
Animal Kingdom, 21, 26, 40
Arcana Calestia, 29
Aristotelian method, 13
Aristotle, 10
Assessor of the Board of Mines, 8

Bacon, F, 10, 20, 27
Behmen, J, 5, 27, 45, 53
Boerhaave, H, 14
Bramins, 3
Brunswicks, 7
Brunswick, Duke of , 8
Bunyan, J, 5
Burns, R, 50

Caesar, J, 33
Casella, 37
Charles XII, 8, 9
Charon, 44

Cicero, 44
Clissold, A, 21
Conjugial Love, 37, 38
Correspondences, 14, 26
Count Hopken, 9
Cristierns, 7

Daedalus Hyperboreus, 8
Dante, A, 37, 47
Deity, 15, 49
Descartes, R, 13
doctrine of Correspondence, 14,
doctrine of Forms, 14
doctrine of Influx, 14
doctrine of Series and Degrees, 14
Duke of Brunswick, 8

*Economy of the Animal
    Kingdom*, 14
Eden, 38
Eleusinian Mysteries, 43
erysipelas, 49

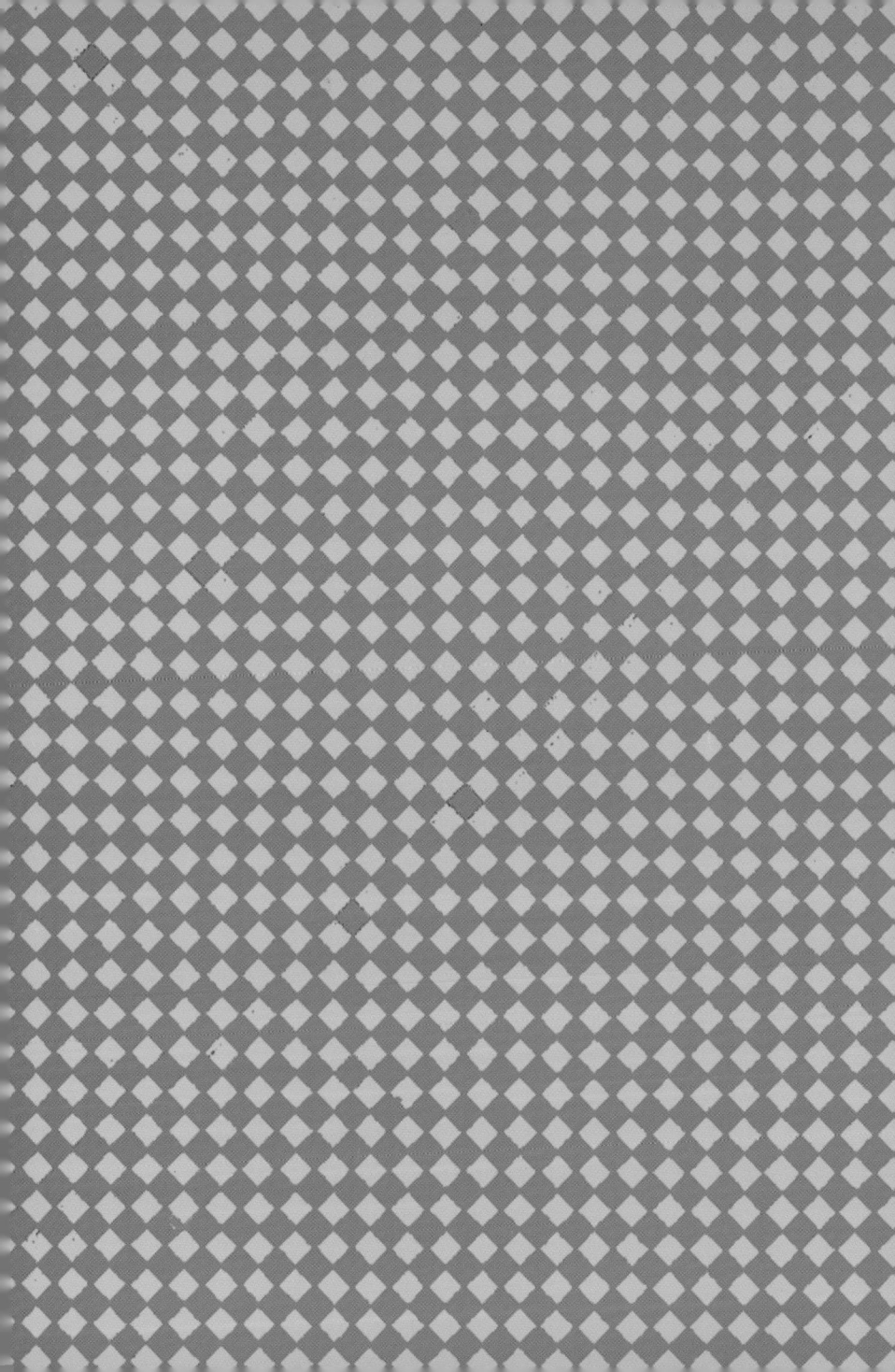